Caution, D

Laura Kester Duerrwaechter

Copyright @2023 by Laura Kester Duerrwaechter

ISBN: 9798867959227
First Edition

All rights reserved. No part of this book may be reproduced or transmitted in any form or by any means, electronic or mechanical, including photocopying, recording or by an information storage or retrieval system, without written permission from the author, except for the inclusion of brief quotations in critical articles and review.

Interior Layout and Design: Laura Kester Duerrwaechter
Cover art: Angela Yuriko Smith

Published in the United States of America
Books available on Amazon.com

Preface

We are born into death. We are forcefully birthed into the unfamiliar surroundings of light and we work steadily through this temporary existence to return to the dark.

I am an observer. - Laura

Table of Contents

Section I – Invitation — 1

Ego's Dying Wish	2
Depth Perception	3
An Empath's Denial	4
Absolution	5
Masquerade	6
Tree of Life	7
The Attending	8

Section II - Stay Awhile — 9

A Mirror's Curse	10
Ascension	11
Gazing	12
Justification	13
Morning Moratorium	14
Cells	15
Vitality Dying	16
Soul Sister	17
A Human Condition	18

Section III - Time to Go — 19

Complacency	20
Undone	21
Caterpillar's Proclamation	22
Observation	23
Unburdened	24
Conflicted Dying	25
Simple Process	26
Puppeteer	27
Author Biography	28

Section I
Invitation

We are born into death; delivered into the state of perpetual ignorance. If we pause and look deeply, each breath we take discounts the final tally.

Ego's Dying Wish

The procession lasted
sixty years.
More or less.

Streets and bridges above
were lined and spectators
stood
uncomfortable at the news
and every shoe was polished.

Vanity watched
from every store front and
could not see her reflection.

Strangers recognized
other strangers for they had
played their roles
brilliantly -
and there was no standing ovation.

The hearse
in somber celebration
and the casket spray overflowed
through the curtained windows.

Late was the morning.
Weighted sighs obscured
by the fog and
I did not remember

Who I used to be.

Depth Perception

I am shallow.

If I lived
deeply-
enough to understand -
the gift of awareness
would conquer my fear.

I am shallow.

If I lived
deeply –
in the light of unknowning,
the gift of awareness
would hold me safe from harm.

I am shallow.

If I lived
deeply –
and a solitary breath promised nothing,
the gift of awareness
would awaken in me
a magical thinking.

I am shallow.

If I lived
deeply –
I would believe
it was meant to be.

An Empath's Denial

Klingon mind-meld
is real.

It happens between him and me.
Unification of two disparate souls
on an uneven playing field.
Life is just that way.

Constant depletion and replenishment
in the dying embers
of a newlywed's dreams -
too long ago.

I will play my part
in this complicit entanglement
of contracted nuptials -
until desire abates and
breath no longer visits.

Life is just that way.

Absolution

Silly human,
what makes you feel
that the turn
of the calendar page
is a cure
for the atrocities you have committed?

Silly human,
what makes you think that space and time
are the tools
of future generations
to be used in reparation
and hope?

Silly human,
What makes you sense that the interconnectedness
of universal life
is merely a curiosity to be conquered?
Forgotten –
within the encasements of museums
and vaults of steel.

Silly human,
Awaken from this dream.

The Masquerade

Death has come
to visit
and try me on
for size.

Each corner I am turning,
I look straight into
the eyes
of one most haunting

And yet -
familiar.

The parts of me
I gave away
are back and
so ill-fitting;
belonging to another me.

So long away
I can't remember.
Let me slumber and
awaken where the fog
denies the hopeful heart.

Tree of Life

Ancient roots
upward -
bursting through soil and
decomposed things.

Twisted and gnarled bark
where imprisoned rings
keep secrets.

Limbs and branches
surviving the storms
of fate.
And each spring, a single leaf
unfolds.

And therein
breathes my soul.
Flexible through time.

The Attending

Death dressed the bride
in sacrificial finery
and she was unaware

Ritual consumed her.
Blinded by ambition.
Timing and all the guests
were present.

An affectation of calm
before the storm.
Upheaval of dreams – cracked and sliding
through a false foundation.

Vows written.
Spoken.
And she was never the same.

Section II
Stay Awhile

Life and death. Each moment precedes and follows; constant upheaval and relief. The soul does not forget. The scars, however, lessen through time as memories are stretched beyond reality. There is no proof and the record keeping is flawed.

A Mirror's Curse

I cut my hair
to look unlike
myself anymore.

I will step into
this curious
rediscovery
in ferocious baby steps.

Innocent curiosity
and delightfulness
in my mental chatter –
a voice I used to know.

A moment's glance
and the reflection is free
to become something
or nothing at all.

Ascension

Come play with me
where the dead
and dying are peacefully
among their peers.

Leave behind the rainbows
and stars   -
where dreams unfold
into ribbons
of broken promises.

Break free
the tethers of awakening.
There is nothing beyond
this moment.

Embrace the destiny
of unity consciousness.
There is no hierarchy in hell.

Gazing

My door frame
frames a door frame
through which the laced curtain
frames a window.

The sunlight filters through
and greets the solitary plant,
so purposefully centered on the sill.

My gaze is interrupted
by the age old glass -
worn and crackled by time
and
my unwillingness to wash it.

He lays in the next room
mostly alive and his breathing
heavily burdened by life choices.

I lay in my bed
under the bedclothes of yellow and powder-blue quilts
without a care in the world.
I don't know why
I am content.
But, I am.

Justification

Deterioration -
It is lovely to watch.
Slowly un-flowering in layers
of dead and dying tissue
left behind in the linens
heaped in piles to wash.

Hour by hour –
assisting in the mundane tasks
of his recovery.

Observing a corpse
struggling to break free
from a life lived in
ignorance of its fragileness.
I watch him – die.

But perhaps,
I will expire first.

Morning Moratorium

The declaration came
at the moment of darkness dying.
Interrupting the other life
I live behind my eyelids.

Happy or raging against the world -
I create the purposeful release
and it keeps me
adrift in the hours
of restless sleeping.

The winged harbinger,
nesting in the tree outside my window,
does little to convince me
in joining her on this new day.

My soul,
in preferential resistance,
remains between
the living layers
of momentary existence.

And if I awaken
fully,
it does not matter.
Time does not exist.

Cells

The purpose of skin
eludes me.
It keeps me in.

I am mummified
and breathing.

Where I must connect
I cannot.
The boundary of atomic
nothingness
separates me -
always.

How futile
to be
more
than what I am.

Alone.

Vitality Dying

The unending sameness
colors my world
in the softness of neutral palettes.
Variations are the lost hope
through which my tired eyes blink the tears dry.

I exist in the sepia tones
and sometimes multitudes of grayness.
Life was simpler then.
Imagination was the rainbow
in my paint box.

Safe in the threshold
of black to white,
my secrets are
buried in luminal spaces where time capsules
do not fit.

Eternity is played out
in the haunting photographs
of someone who used to be me.

Soul Sister

Melancholia
was at my heart's door
as she very often is.

Dressed in memories
I keep in a trunk.
A story woven in
threads and I can't remember.

She has a favorite chair
next to mine
And we share the view
through the window.

Gazing does not change
the inevitable moment
of approaching duskiness
upon a blurry horizon.

We blink.
Tears clear the debris
of hopefulness.

A Human Condition

When we despair -
the connection we seek
cannot be
to the soul of another.

The wrongness
lies imprisoned
underneath the layers
of whom we want
to be

Let go for the other
shall greet the grim reaper
on his own terms.
Unburdened by the selfishness
of our own salvation.

Take the journey.
Honor each misstep
for they are not
meant as a detour.

They are the reason
you are here.

Section III
Time to Go

We each experience moments when Death comes softly; sometimes she comes to cleanse and clear spaces for rebirth. Other times Death comes heavily, striking down the unrelenting ego. Our senses recognize her approach and if given the grace of time, we prepare.

Complacency

He should be dead
by now.

I've dreamed it.
I've manifested it
and am not surprised
that I am still waiting.

Agony, as well as other emotions
are not well-fitted
to a timeline or
or discussion, for that matter.

The observer within
has seen it coming.
He participates involuntarily
denying me release.

Choices on my heart's horizon
battle for the decision
to stay
or go.

And in between
my destiny waits.

Undone

Something is reaching
through me-
wretched and
clumsily twisting;
relenting for release.

Indefinable and
separate from definition.

I could befriend it
and keep it always.

I probably will.

Death is so
unbecoming
upon my lips of rosy tincture
even as —
the coffin is sealed.

Caterpillar's Proclamation

I wish you well
on your journey
for I cannot
go with you.

I must remain
where embers smolder
and the chrysalis was spun
too close to the flame.

Remember me
in fiery profile –
against all odds
and, for a moment
I was glorious.

I am content
in the ash
of what was never
meant to be.

Observation

Seepage -
flowing beneath
temporary layers
of fibers.

The skin of younger days
snuggled against his muscles.
Tendons and ligaments
in disarray of purpose.

Eyes, still hopeful
in moments of focused compliance.
And yet,
he is willing
to live another day.

Unburdened

Your burden
is no longer mine.
I am unwilling.

Your burden
must remain
pristine and festering -
messy and
singularly yours.

Your burden
defines the polarity
of your weakness.

I am strong enough
for me.

Your burden
is no longer mine.
I am unwilling

and
closing the door.

Conflicted Dying

There is a yearning
to know less
within my heart.

The battle rages
and my mind
soldiers on
wearing the chainmail of memories
to immortalize the long dead.

Renewal -
the loss of familiar
and everything
raised in a toast
to sacrificial moments
of here and now.

The letting of blood
as the blade of trust
tenderly severs
and the ego is
lain to rest.

Simple Process

The dying of
the natural world
is preparation.

The dying of
the natural world
is cosmic and messy.
Implosion will
eradicate all fears
and hopefulness.

The dying of
the natural world
is false –
as transmutation
defines reality.

The dying of
the natural world
does not limit
my survival-
having witnessed the same
through all time.

I am eternal
and
already dead.

Puppeteer

I went to bed -
dead.
Painlessly.
Listlessness shifted
into a nothingness, heavy upon the pillow.

Bed bugs feasting.
Winged and patient predators
gazing though streams of moonlight.
Stretching to reach the carrion
tucked in snuggly against the chill.

Evidence of a life
wanes against
now empty spaces -
Once desirous of comfortable places
and memories to share.

Cosmic waves
sparkling in layers
beckoning me come play.
Home again
where marionettes dance
the ballet of life.

Author Biography

Laura Kester Duerrwaechter has been an Indie Pub author since 2017. Her complete collection of poetry chapbooks are among the six million poems curated at the University of Arizona Poetry Center. Some of her earliest books are in circulation at Northwest Florida State College. In addition to poetry, her works, including speculative fiction, short story collections, and memoirs give her a versatile perspective on the written word.

Laura promotes creative writing and volunteers her time mentoring young people who have not been exposed to the process. She is an adjunct professor at Northwest Florida State College and conducts creative writing classes for military members at the local U S Air Force installations near her.

Her work can found on Amazon, in *Space and Time* magazines and in the Christmas Lites anthologies.

Made in the USA
Columbia, SC
28 October 2024